ACHIEVING YOUR PERSONAL BEST

UNLOCKING THE MINDSET, HABITS, AND STRATEGIES FOR A FULFILLING LIFE

FLAVIA ELDEMIRE

Copyright © 2025 by Flavia Eldemire

All rights reserved. No part of this publication may be reproduced, distributed, or transmitted in any form or by any means, including photocopying, recording, or other electronic or mechanical methods, without the prior written permission of the author, except in the case of brief quotations used in reviews, articles, or other noncommercial uses permitted by copyright law.

Disclaimer

This book is a work of nonfiction based on the author's subjective experiences, insights, and opinions. The information provided is for inspirational and educational purposes only. The author and publisher make no guarantees about results and refuse any liability for the use or misuse of this material.

DEDICATION

To my beautiful grandchildren, you are my joy, my inspiration, and my living reminder that purpose flows from generation to generation.

Each of you brings a special light into my life. Your laughter, curiosity, and unconditional love fill my heart with renewed strength every day. As you grow, I pray that you always know how deeply you are loved, how limitless your potential truly is, and how boldly you can walk into your own greatness.

May this book stand as a legacy of encouragement for you — a reminder that you can dream with courage, rise with confidence, and become everything God created you to be. You are the future. You are the hope. You are my heart.

This is dedicated to you, with all my love.

ACKNOWLEDGMENTS

To my beloved family and dear friends — thank you. Your unwavering love, encouragement, and faith have been the quiet strength behind every page of this book. Thank you for believing in me long before I fully believed in myself. Thank you for every prayer, every conversation, every gentle push, and every moment of grace. You reminded me that dreams are nurtured in community, and that even the most ambitious goals are built on the foundation of unconditional support.

To my family — your love has been my anchor and my compass. You taught me resilience, humility, and the power of standing tall in purpose. Every milestone in my life has your fingerprints on it.

To my friends — you have shown up for me with loyalty, laughter, wisdom, and light. Thank you for holding space for my ideas, celebrating my wins, and encouraging me during the long, quiet hours of writing and revising.

To my coaching partners, thank you for your support and for creating a space that allowed me to move beyond my fears. A very special thank you to Dr. Toyletta Riley, for our numerous late-night conversations during the final stages of writing this book, and for encouraging me to think of diverse readers.

This book is not just my achievement. It is ours.

Thank you for being the heart behind *Achieving Your Personal Best*. I pray that I make you proud, and I am forever grateful for each of you.

CONTENTS

Introduction 8

Chapter 1: Introduction to My Personal Best 11

Chapter 2: Self-Awareness as the Foundation for Growth 20

Chapter 3: Vision Crafting: Defining Success on Your Terms 28

Chapter 4: Goal Setting with Intention and Clarity 37

Chapter 5: Cultivating Winning Habits & Daily Routines 48

Chapter 6: Resilience & The Power of Your Environment 58

Chapter 7: Positive Thinking & Affirmations 68

Chapter 8: The Power of Mindset, Affirmations & Reflection 79

Chapter 9: Emotional & Physical Wellness for Peak Performance 87

Chapter 10: Building Support Systems & Accountability Circles 93

Chapter 11: Leading with Purpose & Authenticity 101

Chapter 12: Achieving Your Personal Best: A Lifelong Journey 108

INTRODUCTION

"The only person you are destined to become is the person you decide to be." – Ralph Waldo Emerson

When I first began reflecting on what it truly means to reach my personal best, I discovered something important: it's not about surpassing anyone else; it's about surpassing who I was yesterday. I've had seasons where I felt stuck, unsure, and uncertain about whether my goals were possible. Over time, I realized that becoming my best self isn't a competition; it's a daily choice to rise, even in small ways.

This book isn't filled with complicated theories or lofty language. Instead, it's a heartfelt conversation; just you and me, sharing wisdom, stories, lessons, and the quiet truths that shape real growth. I've learned that personal development unfolds step by step. Sometimes those steps feel heavy, sometimes they feel hopeful, but each one moves you forward.

Achieving Your Personal Best was born from a simple yet powerful belief: every person, regardless of their background, resources, or starting point, has the capacity to rise to their full potential. Not someday. Not when things are perfect. But now. In this very moment.

This book is an invitation to the ambitious heart, the hopeful spirit, and the resilient soul inside you. Whether you're rebuilding, redefining, or reaching higher than ever before, these pages are designed to walk beside you — encouraging you, challenging you, and reminding you of the greatness already within your reach.

Throughout my life and career, I've watched people transform not because they had extraordinary advantages, but because they dared to believe that more was possible. They made the courageous decision to grow. To stretch. To step into their own potential with intention and faith.

As you move through each chapter, you'll uncover insights that help you see yourself more clearly. You'll meet ideas that affirm who you are and inspire who you're becoming. Reaching your personal best isn't about perfection; it's about showing up consistently, offering your best effort, and trusting that growth is always within your grasp.

By the end of this journey, my hope is that you'll not only believe in your ability to change, but also feel empowered to take action, no matter how small those actions may seem. This is your moment to rise, to evolve, and to pursue the highest version of yourself with confidence.

May these pages bring you clarity, courage, and renewed purpose. May they help you reclaim your voice, strengthen your vision, and embrace the truth that excellence is not a destination; it is a daily commitment.

Thank you for allowing me to walk with you on this journey. Let's take the next step together.

CHAPTER 1: INTRODUCTION TO MY PERSONAL BEST

"Your personal best is not about beating others; it's about becoming the person you were meant to be." —Author

Over the years, I've come to realize something that has changed my perspective: success isn't a single goal to reach. It's not a moment when you cross a finish line, take a deep breath, and say, *"I've made it."* It's not just about one big accomplishment that supernaturally makes all your problems disappear.

Success is a journey, not a destination. It involves constantly discovering who you are, learning, growing, and living each day intentionally. I didn't always understand this. There was a time when I believed that working hard to outdo everyone else would bring me fulfillment. I chased titles, recognition, and the kind of success that looks impressive to others. But I soon realized something crucial: even when I "won," I didn't feel like a winner inside.

That's when I realized: **my personal best isn't about competing with others; it's about becoming the truest, strongest, and happiest version of myself** in my mind, in my body, and in my spirit.

This journey is deeply personal. It's about choosing clarity over comparison. It's about staying true to myself instead of seeking approval from people who may not even understand my dreams. And it's about valuing progress more than perfection.

No matter who you are, whether you're a student figuring out your next step, a business owner working hard to create something meaningful, a professional striving for more, or someone who feels there's a deeper purpose to life, I want this book to speak to you because we all have a "personal best" waiting to be discovered.

Chapter 1: Introduction to My Personal Best

WHAT MY PERSONAL BEST MEANS TO ME

My personal best is living in a way that genuinely reflects my values, not the expectations of others. It's waking up with a sense of purpose, setting goals that hold meaning for me, even if they don't make sense to anyone else. It's about finding joy in the process, appreciating the small steps and daily growth, rather than waiting for some "big moment" to finally feel I've learned that my best isn't something fixed; it evolves as I do. There have been times in my life when my best simply meant getting through the day with a positive attitude, and at other times, it meant pushing myself to achieve goals that I once thought were impossible. The key is recognizing that your best will change, and that's perfectly okay.

WHY THIS BOOK MATTERS TO ME

I've read many self-help books over the years. Some inspired me, while others simply echoed the same familiar quotes I'd seen online. The truth is, I wasn't looking for another book that told me what success *should* look like. I was searching for something real.

That's why I'm sharing this from my own life experiences. Every lesson in these pages comes from something I've personally lived through. I've had seasons of doubt, times when I questioned everything, and days when I didn't know how to keep going and wondered if I had what it takes. But I've also experienced the joy of small victories, the quiet pride of realizing I am stronger, braver, and more capable than I thought; moments when I surprised myself with how far I could go. On the following pages, I'll share not just ideas but also real stories. I hope these pages will inspire you to…

- Develop a deeper understanding of yourself.
- Develop a clear vision for your life that motivates and inspires you.
- Create habits that last.
- Stay strong during tough times.
- Take care of your mind and body so you can perform at your highest level.
- Surround yourself with the right people who lift you up instead of pulling you down.

These experiences have influenced my path, and I believe they can influence yours as well.

YOU ARE YOUR BIGGEST PROJECT

One of the most important lessons I've learned is that **I am my best investment**. I can buy many things in life, but nothing is more valuable than the time and energy I invest in becoming a better version of myself.

If professional athletes train every day to reach their peak, why shouldn't we train ourselves for life? Just as they build their strength and refine their skills, we can strengthen our mindset, habits, and emotional health.

I remember a time in my life when I was so focused on work that I forgot to take care of myself. I told myself I didn't have time to eat well, exercise, or rest. But soon, I realized I was running on empty. I was getting sick more often, my mind was foggy, and I lacked motivation. That's when it hit me: I was expecting myself to do my best without giving myself the care I needed.

From that moment, I realized that my well-being was essential. I began with small steps: going to bed earlier, taking short walks, drinking more water, and saying "no" to commitments that drained me. Over time, these small choices boosted my energy, focus, and strength. That's when I understood: I am the foundation of everything I want to achieve.

The Starting Point: Self-Awareness

Before reaching our personal best, we need to understand ourselves first. Self-awareness is like holding a mirror to your life, revealing not only your strengths but also the habits, fears, and thoughts that may be holding you back.

When I started paying attention to myself, I realized I had a habit of reacting quickly when I was upset. This often makes situations worse. But once I became aware of it, I could pause, take a breath, and respond in a way I wouldn't regret later.

Self-awareness helped me set goals that truly resonated with me instead of pursuing those that seemed impressive to others. It also helped me stop negative self-talk and replace it with encouragement. Additionally, it improved my relationships because I could better understand and manage my emotions more effectively.

Confronting the truth about yourself can be difficult, but it's important. Self-awareness is key to genuine growth.

Let me tell you about Maria, a single mother who works full-time as a nurse. She often felt like she was falling short. At work, she poured everything into her patients. At home, she tried to do the same for her son. But by the end of the day, she had nothing left for herself.

One day, Maria realized she was living her life trying to meet everyone else's expectations. She decided to redefine what success meant to her. She no longer aimed to be perfect; she aimed to be present.

She started small. She kept a journal for a few minutes each morning before her son woke up. She took short evening walks with him, enjoying the fresh air and conversation. She began celebrating her small wins, like a good day at work or a peaceful night at home, instead of fixating on what she didn't accomplish.

Over time, Maria felt lighter, happier, and more in control. She realized that success wasn't about doing more; it was about living more intentionally.

The Beginning of the Journey

You are about to start something significant. You have the ability to remove limits, stop following others' rules, and discover your true potential.

Your personal best isn't about being perfect. It's about becoming the version of yourself you'll be proud of, someone who tries, learns, grows, and keeps moving forward.

If you're ready, let's begin this journey together. The truth is, your best life isn't somewhere far off; it starts right here, right now, with the choices you make today.

Chapter 1: Introduction to My Personal Best

Romans 12:2 (NIV) And be not conformed to this world: but be ye transformed by the renewing of your mind, that ye may prove what is that good, and acceptable, and perfect, will of God.

TED Talk:

The Power of Vulnerability – Brené Brown

Further Reading Companion

⇒ *The Gifts of Imperfection* – Brené Brown

⇒ *Atomic Habits* – James Clear

⇒ *You Are a Badass* – Jen Sincero

⇒ *The Four Agreements* – Don Miguel Ruiz

⇒ *Mindset* – Carol Dweck, Ph.D.

CHAPTER 2:
SELF-AWARENESS AS THE FOUNDATION FOR GROWTH

"Knowing yourself is the beginning of all wisdom."
– Aristotle

When I first heard this quote, I thought it was just another nice saying people use to sound deep. Back then, "knowing myself" meant I could list my favorite foods, the music I liked, and that I preferred tea over coffee. But over the years, I realized Aristotle wasn't talking about trivial facts; he was referring to a knowing that changes how you live.

Before I could even consider becoming my best self, I had to slow down and truly understand who I was. That wasn't easy. For a long time, I operated on autopilot; waking up, getting ready, going to work, coming home,

Chapter 2: Self-Awareness as the Foundation for Growth

and collapsing into bed. My life was complete, but it didn't always feel meaningful. I didn't stop to ask myself whether my goals were truly mine or just borrowed from others' expectations.

I thought I was productive, but I was just busy. There's a difference.

Self-awareness isn't just something "nice to have" when you have extra time; it's the foundation for everything. Without it, you can live a life that doesn't feel like yours. I've seen it happen to friends and coworkers: people working tirelessly toward a dream, only to realize years later it wasn't their dream at all.

As I became more self-aware, I started making choices that aligned with my values instead of seeking approval. I recognized the beliefs that quietly held me back, like the idea that asking for help meant I was weak, and I began replacing them with ones that encouraged growth.

It's not that my life suddenly became easy. Problems still appeared, but I could see them more clearly. Instead of just reacting, I could pause, understand what was happening inside me, and respond intentionally. That's a superpower.

One of my biggest breakthroughs in self-awareness happened when I was in a job that seemed perfect on paper. The salary was good, the benefits were excellent, and people often told me I was lucky. But every Sunday night, my chest felt heavy when I thought about Monday morning.

One day, during a particularly stressful week, I asked myself: *"If I removed everyone else's opinions from the equation, would I still choose this life?"*

The answer was a painful *no*.

That answer scared me because it meant I had to make changes I wasn't ready for. But it also set me free. It encouraged me to start asking deeper questions about my values, passions, and the kind of person I wanted to become. That was my first big lesson in self-awareness: sometimes, the life you're living isn't wrong; it's just not yours.

EMOTIONAL AWARENESS AND GROWTH

Part of self-awareness is recognizing your emotions before they take control. I used to think emotions were like the weather, completely outside my influence. Now I see them more like road signs. They aren't good or bad; they're just information.

If I feel frustrated, it's usually because something I care about is being challenged. If I feel anxious, it might be because I'm stepping outside my comfort zone or because I'm ignoring a deeper need.

One pattern I noticed was how defensive I became when someone gave me feedback. At first, I thought it was because I didn't like criticism. But the real reason? I was afraid that feedback meant I wasn't enough. Once I understood that, I could respond differently. Instead of shutting down, I started listening and even asking for feedback. My relationships improved almost instantly.

Society tells us success is about money, titles, and recognition. And while there's nothing wrong with those things, they can feel empty if they don't match what's really important to you.

I remember sitting in a coffee shop once, watching an older man reading a book while slowly sipping his drink. He looked peacefully at the sight of the phone — no rush to be anywhere. I thought to myself, *That's success too*. It's not flashy, but it's real.

So, I asked myself: *If nobody was watching, how would I live my life?*

My answer was simple: I'd spend more time with loved ones, work on projects that inspire me, and live each day intentionally. Once I defined success for myself, I stopped comparing my progress to others. I started judging it by how aligned I felt, not by how impressive my accomplishments seemed.

THE GROWTH MINDSET

Self-awareness also showed me that I am a work in progress, and that's a good thing. For years, I used to see my weaknesses as flaws I needed to hide. Now, I see them as areas for growth. Mistakes aren't proof of failure; they're proof that I'm growing and learning.

Chapter 2: Self-Awareness as the Foundation for Growth

There was a time when I avoided trying new things because I was afraid of failing. But once I adopted a growth mindset, failure became less of a judgment and more of a learning opportunity. If something didn't work out, it didn't mean I was "not good enough." It just meant I'd discovered one more way that didn't work, and I could try again.

I once met a man named Walter. He had spent years working in a corporate job, moving up the ladder. One day, he told me, "I realized I was climbing a ladder that was leaning against the wrong wall."

His words hit me hard. Self-awareness helps you recognize when your ladder is leaning against the wrong wall and gives you the courage to move it, even if you're halfway up.

Here's how I stay grounded:

- **Morning intention** – I spend a few minutes deciding how I want to show up that day.
- **Emotional check-ins** – When I feel a strong emotion, I pause and ask myself, "What's going on here?"

- **Evening reflection** – Before going to sleep, I reflect on whether I have behaved according to my values.

These small habits don't take much time, yet they've made a meaningful difference in my life. They help me recognize when I'm starting to drift away from the path I truly want to be on.

The more self-aware I become, the easier it is to live in harmony with my values. When I am aligned, I feel lighter. My decisions are clearer, my relationships are deeper, and my goals seem more meaningful.

Self-awareness doesn't mean having everything figured out. It just means being willing to keep asking questions, keep observing, and keep growing.

You don't need all the answers right now. The moment you start paying attention to your thoughts, your feelings, and your habits, you've already taken the first step toward becoming your best self.

Chapter 2: Self-Awareness as the Foundation for Growth

Psalm 139:23-24 (KJV) Search me, O God, and know my heart: try me, and know my thoughts: And see if there be any wicked way in me, and lead me in the way everlasting.

TED Talk:

The Power of Self-Awareness – Dr. Tasha Eurich

Further Reading Companion

- ⇒ *Emotional Intelligence 2.0* – Bradberry & Greaves
- ⇒ *The Mountain Is You* – Brianna Wiest
- ⇒ *Leadership & Self-Deception* – Arbinger Institute
- ⇒ *The Laws of Human Nature* – Robert Greene
- ⇒ *What Happened to You?* – Perry & Oprah

CHAPTER 3:
VISION CRAFTING: DEFINING SUCCESS ON YOUR TERMS

"Your vision will become clear only when you can look into your own heart." — **Carl Jung**

I remember the day I first asked myself, *"What does success mean to me?"* It was a quiet Sunday afternoon. I was sitting by the window with a notebook, staring at a blank page. My mind was flooded with all the definitions I'd heard over the years: titles, money, a certain kind of house, recognition, even the way my life "should" look by a certain age. And yet… none of them felt like mine.

It hit me that I'd been chasing a version of success that wasn't really mine: it was shaped by everyone else's expectations. That realization was both uncomfortable

Chapter 3: Vision Crafting: Defining Success on Your Terms

and freeing. It meant I needed to start fresh and define my own terms. This is exactly what this chapter is about: reclaiming the power to decide what success really means for *you*.

Life without a clear vision is like sailing without a compass; you move forward, but you don't know where you're headed. You might cover a lot of ground, but there's no guarantee you'll end up somewhere you want to be.

When your vision is clear and aligned with your purpose.

- You know what matters most, and stop wasting energy on what doesn't.
- You find it simpler to block out distractions.
- You feel more fulfilled, even in difficult times.
- Your decisions begin to make sense because they all point in the same direction.

Having a vision changed how I start my mornings, what I focus on, and who I choose to spend my time with. It became my North Star, guiding every decision.

Living according to someone else's vision is exhausting. It's like wearing clothes that don't fit; no matter how many times you tug or adjust, they still never feel right.

I once had a job that looked good on paper. The title impressed others, the salary was solid, and I seemed to be "on track." But inside, I felt drained. Every day, it felt like I was playing a part in someone else's story. It took me months to realize I wasn't failing at the job; I was failing at being myself.

The pivotal moment happened when I asked:

- *If no one was watching, what would I be doing with my life?*
- *What would make me feel proud even if no one clapped for me?*

That's when I began creating a vision that was uniquely mine.

Your vision is more than just a list of goals; it's a picture of the life you want to live, how you want to feel, and the kind of person you want to become.

Chapter 3: Vision Crafting: Defining Success on Your Terms

When I created my first vision statement, I didn't concentrate on specifics like "owning a house by the beach" or "earning six figures." Instead, I emphasized how I wanted my days to feel: unhurried, purposeful, creative, and connected to the people I love. That shift made all the difference.

A SIMPLE FORMULA FOR A VISION STATEMENT

Here's my process for creating a vision statement:

1. **Start with your feelings.** How do you usually feel? Peaceful? Energized? Free?
2. **Add a clear purpose.** What do you hope to contribute to the world or those around you?
3. **Include details about your lifestyle.** Where do you want to live? How do you want to spend your days?
4. **Anchor it in your core values.** What principles guide you: kindness, growth, creativity, and honesty?

Here's my current one:

I live a life full of creativity and connection, inspiring others through my work, daily growing in wisdom, and appreciating each day with gratitude and peace.

It's brief, but it keeps me grounded.

THE POWER OF VISUALIZATION

One of the most powerful tools I've found for staying true to my vision is visualization. I do it most mornings before checking my phone. I close my eyes and imagine myself living that vision: how my space looks, how my mornings feel, the work I'm doing, and the people I'm with.

At first, it seemed silly, but over time, my mind started accepting that vision as familiar, and I instinctively made choices that led me toward it.

You don't need to visualize for hours; just a few minutes each day will suffice. The key is to feel it, not just see it.

Here's something I wish I had known earlier: not everyone will see or support your vision. And that's okay.

Chapter 3: Vision Crafting: Defining Success on Your Terms

When I told a few people I was leaving my stable career to follow a path that better aligned with my values, I received a mix of reactions; some supportive, others doubtful. At first, it hurt. But I realized that my vision doesn't need everyone's approval to be valid.

Protecting your vision might involve:

- Limiting how much you share with certain people.
- Saying no to opportunities that look good on the surface but don't feel right deep down.
- Surrounding yourself with people who support you, not those who bring you down.

Your vision is like a seed; it needs the right environment to flourish.

David was a college graduate pursuing a career in law. On paper, he had everything planned out. However, he couldn't shake the feeling that his path wasn't really his own. After some deep reflection, he realized his passion was in mentoring young people.

The transition was tough. Friends and family questioned his choice, and at times, he doubted himself. Still, he stayed committed to his vision. Today, he runs a youth leadership academy and wakes up each day eager to do his work.

David's journey demonstrates that courage and clarity can transform everything.

PRACTICAL STEPS TOWARD ACHIEVING YOUR VISION

1. **Identify your five core values.** These serve as the foundation of your vision.
2. **Define your idea of success** in a single sentence.
3. **Create a vision board** with images, words, and colors that inspire you. Place it somewhere you'll see every day.

Your vision is your responsibility. No one else can create it for you, and the good news is, you can improve it as you grow.

The most important thing is to get started. Don't wait for perfect clarity. Begin with what you know now, and let the rest develop as you go.

Chapter 3: Vision Crafting: Defining Success on Your Terms

I'm committed to creating and living a life that reflects who I truly am, one that honors what I value most and fills each day with joy and purpose.

Chapter 3: Vision Crafting: Defining Success on Your Terms

Habakkuk 2:2 (KJV) And the Lord answered me, and said, Write the vision, and make it plain upon tables, that he may run that readeth it."

TED Talk:

How Great Leaders Inspire Action – Simon Sinek

Further Reading Companion

- ⇒ *The Vision Driven Leader* – Michael Hyatt
- ⇒ *Start With Why* – Simon Sinek
- ⇒ *The Light We Carry* – Michelle Obama
- ⇒ *Designing Your Life* – Burnett & Evans
- ⇒ *The Alchemist* – Paulo Coelho
- ⇒ *TED: How Great Leaders Inspire Action* – Simon Sinek

CHAPTER 4:
GOAL SETTING WITH INTENTION AND CLARITY

"Setting goals is the first step in turning the invisible into the visible." — **Tony Robbins**

A clear and intentional goal is one of your most powerful tools. It turns vague desires into focused action, transforms dreams into plans, and bridges the gap between where you are and where you want to be. But here's the truth: not all goals bring fulfillment. Many people set goals based on societal norms, family expectations, or fleeting trends. They chase titles, incomes, or awards without asking the deeper question: *"Do I actually want this, or do I just think I should want this?"*

When we set goals that don't align with who we truly are, we often feel drained, frustrated, or strangely empty, even after "achieving" them. The trophy stays on the shelf, the paycheck goes up, the LinkedIn post gets likes, but deep down, there's a whisper: *Is this all there is?*

To achieve your personal best, you must learn to set goals with **intention and clarity,** goals that are deeply aligned with your vision, values, and sense of purpose.

The Difference Between Ordinary Goals and Purpose-Driven Goals

Ordinary goals are usually reactive. They are established due to pressure, comparison, or habit. For example:

- I should get a larger house because that's the "next step."
- I want to get a specific job title because everyone else my age has it.
- I should lose weight because people expect me to look a certain way.

Purpose-driven goals, however, originate from within. They reflect your true self. They:

- Align with your **long-term vision** for your life.
- Reflect your **core values**.
- Foster lasting dedication rather than temporary motivation. Generate a sense of meaningful progress even before the goal is fully achieved.

When you connect your goals to your purpose, they stop being just checkpoints and start becoming expressions of who you're becoming. Even setbacks take on a different meaning; they become part of your growth rather than proof of failure.

A vague goal leads to ambiguous results. "I want to be successful" is a wish, not a goal.

Clarity turns aspirations into actionable steps. Every clear goal has a definitive answer:

- What exactly am I searching for?
- Why does this matter to me?
- When will I get it done?
- How can I measure my success?

When your goals are clear, you shift from *hoping* to *knowing*. You can create effective strategies, track progress, and make adjustments with confidence. Without clarity, you end up acting randomly but not necessarily making progress in the right direction.

Think of it as sailing. Without a clear destination, you might keep moving but still get lost at sea. Clarity is your compass.

BREAKING BIG GOALS INTO MICRO-WINS

One reason people give up on their goals is that they feel overwhelmed. They set a large goal, notice the gap between where they are and where they want to be, and end up feeling stuck. The solution? Break your big vision into small, manageable steps that build steady momentum. For example:

Vision: Author a book.

Main goal: Complete the first draft within four months.

Micro-Goals:

- Week 1: Create an outline.
- Week 2: Write 1,000 words.

Chapter 4: Goal Setting with Intention and Clarity

- Week 3: Complete Chapter One.

Every small win builds confidence. You train your brain to link your goal with progress and success, which motivates more action.

Micro-goals aren't just about getting things done; they're about shaping who you are. Every small step reinforces the belief: *"I am the kind of person who follows through."*

Motivation can be unpredictable. It's easily influenced by mood, weather, stress, or how much sleep you got the night before. Relying solely on motivation is like depending on sunshine for energy; it works sometimes, but not every day.

Commitment, on the other hand, is a decision. It is the promise you make to yourself to take action, no matter how you feel in the moment.

People who consistently achieve their goals aren't usually the ones who feel motivated every day. They're the ones who show up even when they don't feel like it.

Here are some ways to reinforce your commitment:

- Reflect on your "why" every morning.

- Build accountability through mentors, partnerships, or public obligations.
- Focus on discipline as a muscle: the more you use it, the stronger it becomes.

DISCIPLINE: THE BRIDGE TO ACHIEVEMENT

Jim Rohn said, *"Discipline is the bridge between goals and accomplishment."*

Discipline isn't about strict control; it's about creating a structure that fosters your growth. When you swap out the question *"Should I do this today?"* with *"This is what I do every day,"* you save mental energy and increase your chances of success.

Athletes don't train only when they feel inspired. Writers don't write only when the words come easily. Successful entrepreneurs don't work only when it's convenient. They have systems, routines, and non-negotiables that keep them moving forward.

The same principle applies to you. Your goals shouldn't rely on perfect conditions. A routine of daily, repeatable actions should support them.

Chapter 4: Goal Setting with Intention and Clarity

A common reason people feel unfulfilled after reaching a goal is that the goal itself wasn't aligned with their core values. You might achieve something impressive in others' eyes, but still feel empty if it's not connected to what matters most to you.

If one of your core values is **freedom**, but your goal requires you to work 80-hour workweeks forever, you might achieve it, but at the expense of your happiness.

If one of your values is **connection**, but your goal separates you from the people you love, the achievement will feel empty.

Before setting a goal, ask yourself:

- Does this bring me closer to the life I truly want?
- Will accomplishing this make me proud, not just now but years from now?
- Am I pursuing this because it excites me, or because I think I "should"?

Once you set a clear goal, you must safeguard it from both outside distractions and your self-sabotage.

External distractions include new "shiny" opportunities that draw your attention away. Internal distractions involve doubts, procrastination, or perfectionism.

Protecting your goal means:

- Saying "no" to opportunities that don't match your current priorities.
- Establishing boundaries to preserve your time and energy.
- Remembering that not everything urgent is essential.

Every goal has a price. Achieving it often requires sacrificing something else, such as leisure, other projects, or specific habits. The clearer you are about your priorities, the easier it becomes to make those trade-offs.

Elena, a working mother of two, had always dreamed of starting her wellness coaching business. But balancing her career, parenting duties, and household chores made the dream seem overwhelming and nearly unreachable.

Instead of attempting a large leap all at once, Elena focused on small goals.

Chapter 4: Goal Setting with Intention and Clarity

- **First:** She dedicated a week to researching certifications.
- **Next:** She spends 30 minutes each evening studying.
- **Then:** She began reaching out to people in her network to find potential clients.

These steps were small enough to fit into her busy life but meaningful enough to propel her forward. Within a year, she had achieved her dream career not through a single big leap, but by consistently taking small, deliberate steps aligned with her vision.

Her story shows that you don't need big moves to change your life. Consistent, meaningful actions driven by clarity and purpose are what make the difference.

Short-term goals are important, but if they aren't linked to a larger vision, they can result in aimless progress and reaching targets that don't matter in the long run.

Think of your goals as parts of a bigger story. Each one is a chapter, and how you pick them shapes your life's path. When you step back and see how your current goals fit into your 5-, 10-, or 20-year vision, you gain perspective. You become more patient with setbacks and more strategic about your actions.

Chapter 4: Goal Setting with Intention and Clarity

Proverbs 21:5 (KJV) The thoughts of the diligent tend only to plenteousness; but of every one that is hasty only to want.

TED Talk:

Grit – Angela Duckworth

Further Reading Companion

- ⇒ *The One Thing* – Gary Keller
- ⇒ *Essentialism* – Greg McKeown
- ⇒ *Grit* – Angela Duckworth
- ⇒ *The 12 Week Year* – Moran & Lennington
- ⇒ *High Performance Habits* – Brendon Burchard
- ⇒ *Dream Big and Live Your Dreams Boldly: Taking Action to Fulfill Your Passion and Purpose--* Kwende, Maurine

CHAPTER 5:
CULTIVATING WINNING HABITS & DAILY ROUTINES

"We are what we repeatedly do. Excellence, then, is not an act, but a habit." —**Aristotle**

I've learned that success doesn't come from a single big moment of glory or just one lucky break. It's not about doing something grand once and then relaxing, expecting everything else to fall into place. True success is built on the small things you do every day, the quiet habits that nobody might even notice but that shape you into the person you're becoming.

Every decision I make adds up over time. When I decide to work on my craft instead of scrolling through my phone, I am voting for the person I want to become. When I take a walk instead of lying on the couch, I reinforce my identity as someone who values health. And when I choose not to focus on distraction, I am showing myself commitment to my goals.

These small actions may seem minor at first, but they create momentum. Over weeks, months, and years, they form the foundation of everything you accomplish. I've seen this happen in my own life, not because I'm perfect, but because I've learned to turn small wins into a habit.

THE IDENTITY-HABIT CONNECTION: YOU BECOME WHAT YOU DO

Your habits not only reveal what you do but also shape who you are. Every time you repeat an action, you're sending a message to yourself about your identity.

- Every time I sit down to write, I remind myself that *I am a writer.*
- Every time I wake up early to exercise, I remind myself that *I care for my body.*
- Every time I resist the urge to procrastinate, I remind myself that *I am disciplined and committed.*

That's why it's important to look beyond just goals. Goals guide you, but your habits are what truly move you forward. You don't automatically achieve your goals; when the moment arrives, you rely on your habits. If your habits are weak, your results will be weak too.

I used to think I needed to wait for motivation before I could act, but I've learned it's the other way around; action creates motivation. The more you show up and "take action," the more your brain believes, *"This is who I am."* That identity encourages you to keep going.

KEYSTONE HABITS: THE SMALL WINS THAT TRANSFORM EVERYTHING

Not all habits are equal. Some are "keystone habits," small actions that create positive ripple effects in various parts of your life. When you master one of these, everything else becomes simpler.

For me, one of my most important keystone habits is a simple morning workout. It doesn't have to be intense; even a quick 15-minute stretch or a light jog can boost how I feel for the rest of the day. I have more energy,

Chapter 5: Cultivating Winning Habits & Daily Routines

think more clearly, and am in a better mood. That one habit influences how I eat, how I work, and even how I interact with others.

Another important habit I maintain is keeping a daily journal. Spending just 10 minutes each evening writing about my day helps me process my thoughts, reduce stress, and stay focused on my goals. When I journal regularly, I sleep better and make smarter decisions.

Sleep is another important factor. I used to overlook the importance of a consistent bedtime. Now, I protect my sleep as if it were a treasure. When I get quality sleep, my focus sharpens, my patience increases, and my productivity skyrockets.

If you focus on building just a few key habits, you'll notice many other positive changes occur naturally.

One thing I've noticed about high performers is that they don't rely solely on willpower. They cultivate habits that make good decisions automatic.

For me, having a consistent morning routine means I don't waste energy deciding what to do first. I wake up, drink a glass of water, do some stretches, and read a few pages of something inspiring. That routine prepares my mind and body for the day.

During the day, I divide my work into blocks. I focus on my most difficult tasks in the morning when my energy is highest, then switch to lighter work in the afternoon. This helps me align my work with my natural focus cycles instead of fighting them.

In the evenings, I unwind with a routine that tells my brain it's time to rest: dimming the lights, putting away screens, and reading something light. This simple habit helps me fall asleep more quickly and wake up feeling refreshed.

By establishing routines throughout my day, I reduce the number of decisions I have to make. This way, I save my mental energy for creative thinking and problem-solving instead of figuring out what to do next.

Chapter 5: Cultivating Winning Habits & Daily Routines

THE HABIT LOOP: CUE → ROUTINE → REWARD

I've realized that every habit follows a similar pattern: a cycle that begins with a **cue**, then a **routine**, and ends with a **reward**.

For example:

- **Cue:** I place my workout clothes next to my bed.
- **Routine:** I put them on and do my morning workout.
- **Reward:** I enjoy the energy boost after exercising and a good breakfast.

Understanding this loop helps me build habits intentionally. I create strong cues, so my brain recognizes it's time to act, and I ensure there's a meaningful reward that encourages me to repeat the habit.

One of my favorite techniques is habit stacking, which means linking a new habit to something I already do. For example:

- After brushing my teeth in the morning, I repeat three affirmations.

- After pouring my morning coffee, I write down my top three priorities for the day.

These small links help habits stick and lower the chances of skipping them.

One of the main lessons I've learned is that productivity isn't about managing time; it's about managing energy.

I pay attention to my natural rhythms. I know I'm most alert in the morning, so I schedule deep work during that time. I use midday breaks to recharge, whether it's a short walk or a quick stretch. I also respect my body's need to slow down in the evening so I can get quality rest.

When I align with my energy instead of fighting it, I accomplish more in less time and feel better doing it.

I once met a man named Malik, a corporate executive with a busy job and a young family. He was constantly stressed and felt like he was failing both at work and at home.

Chapter 5: Cultivating Winning Habits & Daily Routines

Instead of attempting to change everything all at once, Malik began with small steps. He focused on three habits:

- A dedicated 30-minute work session every morning.
- A 10-minute evening journaling reflection.
- A strict "no phone" rule during family dinner.

At first, these small changes seemed insignificant. But within three months, Malik noticed a major improvement. He was getting more done at work, feeling less overwhelmed, and his relationship with his family became closer.

Malik's story reminded me that we don't need to change our lives all at once. Small, steady actions every day can lead to big results.

- *I use affirmations to empower the person I am becoming.*
- *My habits influence the person I am becoming.*
- *I create routines that ensure success.*
- *Consistent small actions lead to remarkable results.*

Repeating these phrases to myself helps me stay committed, even on days when motivation is low.

I am dedicated to forming daily habits and routines that align with my highest standards. Every small, purposeful step brings me closer to achieving my personal best.

"You do not rise to the level of your goals. You fall to the level of your systems." – **James Clear**

Chapter 5: Cultivating Winning Habits & Daily Routines

Galatians 6:9 (KJV) *And let us not be weary in well doing: for in due season we shall reap, if we faint not.*

TED Talk:

Try Something New for 30 Days – Matt Cutts

Further Reading Companion

- ⇒ *The Power of Habit* – Charles Duhigg
- ⇒ *Atomic Habits* – James Clear
- ⇒ *Discipline Is Destiny* – Ryan Holiday
- ⇒ *Make Your Bed* – Adm. McRaven
- ⇒ *The Miracle Morning* – Hal Elrod
- ⇒ *Everyday Artist: Creating The Life You Want To Live* – Barbara Addison Reid

CHAPTER 6:
RESILIENCE & THE POWER OF YOUR ENVIRONMENT

"Success is not final, failure is not fatal: It is the courage to continue that counts." — *Winston Churchill*

I've learned something about life: no matter how much we try to plan every detail, there will always be moments when things fall apart. A dream doesn't go the way we imagined, an opportunity slips away, or an unexpected storm interrupts us. Those moments can break us or build us. The difference comes down to one thing: **resilience**.

Resilience isn't just about "toughing it out." It's the quiet, steady determination to get back up after being knocked down. It's a choice to grow through the struggle, not just go through it. And here's good news:

Chapter 6: Resilience & The Power of Your Environment

resilience isn't something you're born with or without. It's a skill. Like a muscle, it gets stronger the more you use it.

But I've also learned something else: resilience doesn't develop in isolation. Your environment, the people around you, the places where you live and work, and the energy you welcome into your life can either drain you or help you bounce back quicker. If resilience is the engine that keeps you moving forward, then your environment is the road you're traveling on. A smooth, clear path can make the journey much easier.

This chapter covers both developing inner resilience and creating an external environment that fosters it.

REDEFINING FAILURE: THE FEEDBACK THAT SHAPES US

For years, I viewed failure as a sign of weakness. When things didn't succeed, I blamed myself. I believed it meant I wasn't good enough, smart enough, or capable enough. But the more I studied people I admired, such as entrepreneurs, athletes, leaders, and creators, the more I realized they all shared one thing in common: they had failed, often spectacularly.

The difference was that they didn't view failure as the end; they saw it as feedback.

A failed plan can reveal where your assumptions were wrong. A lost opportunity can expose a gap in your skills or strategy. A mistake can uncover blind spots you never realized. These aren't punishments; they're valuable lessons you couldn't learn any other way.

So now, when I face a setback, I remind myself: **this isn't the end, it's an opportunity to recalibrate.** I'm gathering data, refining my approach, and building strength for the next attempt.

Being resilient doesn't mean denying that the pain exists. It means facing it head-on without letting it define who you are. I've had nights when I stared at my ceiling, wondering whether I should give up. The turning point always came when I asked a different question instead of *"Why is this happening to me?"* I'd ask, *"What is this teaching me?"*

I also learned to recognize and value small wins, even during tough times. Gratitude became my base. Sometimes, a "win" was showing up. Other days, it was sending that one email I'd been avoiding. These tiny victories gave me the momentum I needed to face bigger challenges later.

And most importantly, I learned to focus on what I could control: my actions, my mindset, and my effort. I can't control how others respond, how quickly things happen, or whether the world throws me another curveball, but I can control how I show up.

MOMENTUM COMES IN MINUTES, NOT MARATHONS

When you get knocked down, the thought of making a big comeback can seem overwhelming. That's why I moved from imagining giant leaps to concentrating on small, manageable steps.

Sometimes, resilience means taking just ten minutes to do something that moves you forward, such as drafting a rough outline for a project. I'm sending a message to a mentor and organizing my workspace to make it feel fresh again. These small actions matter; they remind me that I still have agency, even when life feels chaotic.

Tasha, a friend of mine, serves as a perfect example. She started two businesses, but both failed. She was devastated and thought about quitting altogether. However, instead of giving up, she took a hard look at her situation.

She unfollowed social media accounts that made her feel like she was falling behind. She joined a mastermind group of encouraging, like-minded entrepreneurs. She even redesigned her home office to feel bright, inspired, and aligned with her vision.

Her third business didn't just survive; it thrived. The difference wasn't luck; it was because she eliminated the things draining her energy and replaced them with things that fueled her resilience.

YOUR ENVIRONMENT: THE SILENT INFLUENCER

Here's the truth many people overlook: you can have the best intentions, clear goals, and strong habits, but if your environment works against you, progress becomes an uphill battle.

Chapter 6: Resilience & The Power of Your Environment

Reflect on this. If your workspace is cluttered and noisy, how difficult is it to focus? If your closest friends frequently complain or discourage you, how difficult is it to dream big? If your phone constantly buzzes with notifications, how difficult is it to stay present?

Your environment affects you, whether you notice it or not. Every person you spend time with, every room you enter, and every feed you scroll through either moves you closer to your personal best or pushes you farther away from it.

I view my environment as a stage for my best self. *What would the stage for the next version of me look like?* Then I bring it to life.

That might suggest:

- I've cleared my desk, so now I can sit down and work.
- Listening to music that energizes me when I need a creative boost.
- Scheduling regular coffee chats with inspiring people.

- Establishing "phone-free zones" to resist the urge to scroll endlessly.

It doesn't need to be perfect. It just needs to help me focus on what matters most.

We often discuss "toxic spaces," but toxic relationships can be even more damaging. If someone constantly undermines you, dismisses your dreams, or fills your mind with doubt, your resilience will weaken.

On the other hand, the right people can be your greatest motivation. They remind you of your worth when you forget it. They challenge you to improve when you're tempted to settle. They celebrate your wins, even the small ones, when you're too focused on your failures to notice them yourself.

Over time, I've learned to be intentional about who I let into my inner circle. My energy is too valuable to waste on people who don't respect it.

THE ENERGY FLOW TEST

I often do a quick mental check: "Does this person, space, or activity leave me feeling more energized or

Chapter 6: Resilience & The Power of Your Environment

more drained?" If it's consistently draining me, I either change it or remove it from my life.

This isn't about avoiding challenges that are necessary for growth but about removing unnecessary obstacles. Life already throws enough hurdles at us. We don't need to keep tripping over our own feet.

Resilience and the environment reinforce each other. When your environment is supportive, maintaining resilience becomes easier. Conversely, being resilient enables you to improve your surroundings.

Think of it this way: resilience is your ability to climb mountains, and your environment is the weather you face while climbing. You can climb during a storm, but it's much easier in clear skies. Why not give yourself the best conditions possible?

I've stopped searching for a definitive point in resilience. It's not something you create once and then move on from. It's a lifelong practice. The same goes for your environment; it requires regular check-ins and adjustments as your goals and circumstances evolve.

There will still be setbacks. There will still be failures. But now I see them differently. I understand they're part of the process, not proof that I'm failing in life. I also know I can make choices, both internally and externally, that help me bounce back faster each time.

I'll leave you with the words of J.K. Rowling, who turned her lowest point into the foundation for one of the most successful book series ever: "Rock bottom became the solid foundation on which I rebuilt my life."

Resilience isn't about never falling. It's about how you respond after you fall and whether the environment you create around yourself makes it easier to get back up.

Chapter 6: Resilience & The Power of Your Environment

Isaiah 40:31 (KJV) But they that wait upon the LORD shall renew their strength; they shall mount up with wings as eagles; they shall run, and not be weary; and they shall walk, and not faint.

TED Talk:

The Power of Believing You Can Improve – Carol Dweck

Further Reading Companion

- Option B – Sheryl Sandberg
- The Obstacle Is the Way – Ryan Holiday
- Dare to Lead – Brené Brown
- Thrive – Arianna Huffington
- Will – Will Smith

CHAPTER 7: POSITIVE THINKING & AFFIRMATIONS

"Keep your face always toward the sunshine and shadows will fall behind you." — *Walt Whitman.*

I've realized that my thoughts shape how I live. When I fill my mind with negative thoughts, it feels like my whole life gets heavier, as if I'm carrying an invisible weight that slows me down. But when I choose to think positively, it's like a light turns on inside me, guiding me through even the darkest days. Positive thinking isn't about pretending everything is perfect or ignoring real problems; it's about viewing life in a way that gives me hope, courage, and the strength to keep moving forward.

Chapter 7: Positive Thinking & Affirmations

I remember a time when I faced a big disappointment. I had worked hard for a promotion, putting in extra hours and doing more than necessary. I believed that the position was mine. But when the decision was announced, they gave it to someone else. My first reaction was frustration and self-doubt. Thoughts like *"I'm not good enough"* and *"Nothing ever works out for me"* flooded my mind. These thoughts made me feel even worse, to the point where I almost wanted to give up.

But then I stopped myself. I decided to change my perspective. Instead of seeing it as a loss, I chose to see it as a lesson and an opportunity to gain experience. I told myself, *"This is not the end. Something better is waiting for me."* That one change in my thinking kept me motivated. A few months later, I got an even better opportunity with another company, something I would have missed if I had let my disappointment turn into bitterness.

That's the thing about positive thinking: it doesn't eliminate life's challenges, but it changes how you respond to them. It helps you see opportunities where others only see problems. When you focus on what's possible, you start to notice doors that have always been there but were hidden by fear or doubt.

Positive thinking is more than just *"being happy"* all the time. It's a daily practice. It involves training your mind to focus on solutions instead of dwelling on problems. When something bad happens, I ask myself:

- *What can I learn from this?*
- *What should I do next?*

These questions help me avoid frustration. They shift my energy from feeling helpless to feeling capable of taking action.

I've noticed that starting my mornings with positive thoughts boosts my entire day. If I wake up grouchy and complain about minor things, I carry that mood with me all day. But when I intentionally tell myself, *"Today is going to be a good day. I'm going to handle whatever comes my way with strength,"* it sets the tone for my mood, my choices, and how I interact with others.

Positive thinking also affects my health. When I have a negative mindset, I feel more tired and stressed. But when I focus on gratitude and hope, I feel lighter and more energized. Science even supports this. Studies show that positive thinking can reduce stress, improve heart health, and boost the immune system.

THE POWER OF AFFIRMATIONS

One of the best tools I've discovered for promoting positive thinking is **affirmation**. Affirmations are short, impactful statements you repeat to yourself to boost your mindset. They work because your brain begins to believe what you consistently say.

If you keep saying, *"I can't do this,"* your mind will seek evidence to support that belief. But if you tell yourself, *"I am capable," "I am strong,"* or *"I am worthy,"* your mind will start to find proof of those instead.

When I first started using affirmations, I honestly felt silly. Standing in front of the mirror saying, *"I believe in myself,"* felt awkward. But I kept at it. Over time, I noticed a change. I walked with more confidence, spoke with more certainty, and stopped letting fear control me.

Some affirmations I often use include:

- I manage my thoughts and feelings.
- I am becoming the best version of myself.
- Opportunities are everywhere around me.
- I deserve happiness and success.
- I have everything I need for success within myself.

I say them in the morning before I start my day and at night before I go to sleep. Sometimes, I write them down in a notebook; writing them makes them feel more tangible and real.

Replacing Negative Thoughts

Positive thinking also involves **replacing** negative thoughts with better ones. It doesn't mean pretending that sad things don't exist; it means not letting them control your mind.

If I make a mistake, my old habit was to say, *"I'm so stupid."* Now, I replace that thought with, *"I made a mistake, but I can fix it and learn from it."* This change greatly boosts my self-confidence and helps me move forward instead of getting stuck in guilt.

Chapter 7: Positive Thinking & Affirmations

I like to think of the mind as a garden. If you let weeds grow — negative thoughts — they'll take over. But if you plant positive thoughts and nurture them, they'll fill the space with beauty. You can't stop weeds from appearing now and then, but you can pull them out before they take over.

The people you spend time with have a significant influence on your mindset. If you're around those who constantly complain or focus only on the negatives, it's more challenging to remain positive. However, if you surround yourself with people who uplift, believe in, and inspire you, your thoughts tend to become more optimistic.

I intentionally spend time with friends, family, and mentors who lift me up instead of bringing me down. I also pay close attention to what I watch, read, and listen to. Social media, news, and entertainment all impact my mindset. I try to nourish my mind with inspiring books, motivational videos, and uplifting stories, not because I ignore reality, but because I prepare myself to face it with strength.

My Daily Positive Thinking Routine

I've created a straightforward routine that keeps me focused on positivity.

- **Morning Gratitude** – Before I get out of bed, I think about three things I am grateful for.
- **Affirmations** – I say three affirmations in the mirror to start my day positively.
- **Positive Practice** – I dedicate at least 10 minutes to reading or listening to something inspiring.
- **Mind Check** – Throughout the day, I watch my thoughts. When I notice a negative one, I replace it with a more positive thought.
- **Evening Reflection** – Before going to bed, I think about one good thing that happened that day, no matter how small.

This simple practice has enabled me to remain calm and focused even during stressful times.

Handling Setbacks Positively

It's easy to stay positive when everything goes smoothly. The real test comes when things fall apart.

Chapter 7: Positive Thinking & Affirmations

I've had days where I wake up feeling motivated and prepared, only for something unexpected to happen: a work project fails, a sudden expense appears, or I get into an argument with someone close.

When that happens, I allow myself to feel my emotions. Positive thinking doesn't mean forcing a fake smile while ignoring your feelings. It means recognizing them and then choosing not to get stuck in them. I might go for a walk, write in my journal, or talk to a trusted friend. Then, I ask myself, *"What can I do next?"* and *"What's the lesson here?"*

Over time, practicing positive thinking and affirmations has transformed me. I'm not saying I never feel fear or doubt, but I bounce back faster when I do. I've learned to see challenges as temporary, failures as lessons, and the future as something I can shape.

I've also noticed that my relationships have gotten better. People are drawn to positive energy and respond more if I speak with hope instead of constant complaining. The biggest change is that I believe in myself more than ever before.

Ultimately, positive thinking and affirmations have become an integral part of my life. They've helped me face challenges with courage, recover from setbacks, and continue moving toward my goals. I still experience bad days, but I know that every day offers me the chance to choose my thoughts. By focusing on the good, I give myself the power to shape a better future.

Chapter 7: Positive Thinking & Affirmations

Philippians 4:8 (KJV) *Finally, brethren, whatsoever things are true, whatsoever things are honest, whatsoever things are just, whatsoever things are pure, whatsoever things are lovely, whatsoever things are of good report; if there be any virtue, and if there be any praise, think on these things.*

TED Talk:

Why Great Leaders Take Humor Seriously - Jennifer Aaker and Naomi Bagdonas

Further Reading Companion

⇒ *The Power of Positive Thinking* – Norman Vincent Peale

⇒ *You Can Heal Your Life* – Louise Hay

⇒ *Think Like a Monk* – Jay Shetty

⇒ *The Magic of Thinking Big* – David Schwartz

⇒ *Battlefield of the Mind* – Joyce Meyer

⇒ *Blessed Assurance: Deep Thought and Meditations in the Tradition and Wisdom of Our Ancestors* — Myers, Linda James

CHAPTER 8:
THE POWER OF MINDSET, AFFIRMATIONS & REFLECTION

"Your mind is a garden. Your thoughts are the seeds. You can grow flowers, or you can grow weeds." — **Unknown**

I've realized that the life I live on the outside always begins with what I cultivate on the inside. My external world reflects my internal thoughts. Every idea I think, every belief I hold, and every word I tell myself influence what happens next.

For years, I believed success was about luck or opportunity. Now I realize it begins with my mindset. When I think of the people I respect most, they all have one thing in common: they carefully guard their thoughts.

A positive mindset doesn't happen by accident. It's not like waking up to find a gift on your doorstep. Instead, it's a daily choice, discipline, and sometimes a challenge. I've had days when my mind felt like a battlefield, with fear on one side and hope on the other. If I don't manage my thoughts, they tend to lean toward doubt, fear, and limitations. But when I take control and intentionally guide my thoughts, everything changes. I feel more in control, more alive, and ready to act.

I've experienced this firsthand myself. On days when I start with intentional thoughts, reminding myself of my worth, highlighting my strengths, and seeing challenges as opportunities, I feel more confident and productive. When I let negativity creep in, I become slower, hesitant, and easily discouraged. The main difference isn't my circumstances; it's my mindset.

THE INNER DIALOGUE SHIFT: FROM CRITIC TO CHAMPION

For a long time, the voice inside my head was my harshest critic. If I made a mistake, I would replay it again. If I tried something new, it would remind me of all the ways it could go wrong.

Chapter 8: The Power of Mindset, Affirmations & Reflection

One day, I asked myself a simple but powerful question: *What if I spoke to myself the way a great coach would?* Imagine that voice encouraging me after every stumble, celebrating small wins, and reminding me of my power even on the worst days. That's when I realized I could train that inner voice.

For me, it started with awareness. I began catching myself in moments of self-criticism, much like I would see a friend making an unfair comment. Then I would pause and ask: *Is this true, or is it just my fear talking?* Many times, it was just emotion, not fact.

From there, I began redefining my thoughts. Instead of saying, "I'll never get this right," I told myself, "*I'm learning and improving every day.*" I anchored those thoughts with affirmations like, "*I am capable and resourceful.*" Over time, I saw my confidence grow, not because life became easier, but because I was becoming my own biggest supporter.

I've studied leaders and high performers for years, and one thing is clear: they protect the stories they tell themselves. They don't let fear have the final say. They don't let a single failure define who they are.

I remember watching an athlete I admire lose a big competition. When asked how he felt, he said, "This is feedback, not the end." That stuck with me. Leaders think differently because they see setbacks as part of the process, not proof they can't succeed.

They also choose possibility over limitation. Even in uncertain situations, they ask, *"What's possible here?"* rather than *"What's going to go wrong?"* and prepare for challenges by using affirmations as a form of mental armor. I've started doing the same before big meetings or difficult conversations, telling myself things like, *"I am calm, confident, and ready."* It changes how I show up.

DEEP DIVE: THE SCIENCE OF SELF-TALK AND SUCCESS

Initially, I believed positive self-talk was just "feel-good talk." But then I discovered the science behind it. Studies in cognitive behavioral therapy demonstrate that how we talk to ourselves directly influences performance, stress resilience, and decision-making.

Chapter 8: The Power of Mindset, Affirmations & Reflection

When I speak positively to myself, my brain releases dopamine, a chemical that boosts motivation and learning. But when I dwell on negative thoughts, my body produces more cortisol, the stress hormone, which clouds my focus and makes me more reactive.

In other words, my self-talk functions like a command system for my brain. When I give it empowering instructions, it acts in my favor. When I feed it fear and doubt, it works against me. Knowing this has made me more intentional than ever about the words I use, even in my own mind.

For years, I moved through life quickly without taking time to reflect. I would jump from one task to the next, one challenge after another, without ever asking, *"What is this teaching me?"*

Now I see reflection as the bridge between experience and wisdom. Without it, we repeat the same mistakes, unaware of the patterns holding us back. Reflection isn't about dwelling on the past; it's about extracting the lessons so I can move forward stronger.

Sometimes I take just five minutes at the end of the day to reflect on what went well, what challenged me, and what I can do better tomorrow. It's amazing how even that small habit sharpens my awareness and helps me continue to grow.

One of the most effective changes I've made is combining affirmations with reflection. In the morning, I stand in front of the mirror, look myself in the eye, and confidently say three affirmations. I visualize myself living through those moments that day.

In the evening, I think about what I learned today. *How did I embody those affirmations?* I write down one empowering belief I reinforced that day. Over time, this creates a loop: I affirm, I act, I reflect, I refine. And with each cycle, I become a little stronger, a little wiser, and much more intentional.

I've noticed that my identity is shaped by the words I repeat about myself. If I keep saying, *"I'm terrible at time management,"* I'll act in ways that prove it. If I say, *"I'm disciplined and focused,"* I start living up to it.

Chapter 8: The Power of Mindset, Affirmations & Reflection

Now, I speak like the person I am becoming. I align my language with my future self, not my past mistakes. Every time I say, "I am," I'm laying a brick in the foundation of my future. That's why I choose those words carefully.

AWARD-WINNING AFFIRMATIONS

I often use affirmations like: "I am the author of my inner narrative, and I choose words of power and possibility." "Each reflection sharpens my awareness and accelerates my growth." "My thoughts are aligned with my highest potential and daily actions." "I am becoming the leader my vision requires." "Every day, I affirm, act, and ascend to greater levels of success."

They may seem simple, but they grow stronger when spoken with confidence every day.

Chapter 8: The Power of Mindset, Affirmations & Reflection

Proverbs 23:7 (KJV) For as he thinketh in his heart, so is he.

TED Talk:

How to Stop Screwing Yourself Over - Mel Robbins

Further Reading Companion

- ⇒ *The Success Principles* – Jack Canfield
- ⇒ *The High 5 Habit* – Mel Robbins
- ⇒ *Inner Engineering* – Sadhguru
- ⇒ *The Untethered Soul* – Michael Singer
- ⇒ *The Four Agreements* – Don Miguel Ruiz
- ⇒ *50 Powerful Mindset: Transform Your Thinking for Business Success* — Demetrice Phillips

CHAPTER 9: EMOTIONAL & PHYSICAL WELLNESS FOR PEAK PERFORMANCE

"Take care of your body. It's the only place you have to live." — *Jim Rohn*

You can have the most detailed goals, the sharpest strategies, and the strongest willpower. Still, without emotional and physical wellness, your ability to perform at your best will always be limited. Your wellness isn't just an accessory to success; it is the foundation.

When you're emotionally or physically drained, everything becomes more difficult: focus, decision-making, creativity, and even discipline. But by taking care of your well-being, you unlock sustained energy, emotional resilience, and a flow of productivity that feels almost automatic.

Your mind and body are always communicating. Emotional stress often causes physical tension, while physical exhaustion can impair mental clarity. Positive emotions can boost energy levels, and physical vitality can improve your thinking. To perform at your best, you need to nurture both aspects of this connection. That's why top performers consider wellness a crucial strategy rather than a luxury or an afterthought.

Emotional Wellness: The Hidden Key to Consistency

Success isn't just about what you do; it's about how you feel while doing it. Unmanaged emotions like stress, anxiety, or frustration become background noise that distracts you and saps your energy. Emotional wellness helps you handle challenges with calmness, creativity, and persistence.

This involves finding ways to restore your emotional balance through quick daily mindfulness exercises, releasing emotional clutter via journaling, and staying

Chapter 9: Emotional & Physical Wellness for Peak Performance

mindful of your inner state by asking yourself throughout the day, "What am I feeling right now, and what do I need?" It also includes protecting your emotional capacity by saying no to things that drain you and yes to those that uplift you. Emotional agility isn't about avoiding feelings; it's about handling them constructively.

Neglecting your body is like trying to run high-performance software on outdated hardware. The core pillars of physical wellness are simple yet often underestimated in impact. Proper nutrition energizes the body and sharpens mental clarity for maximum focus. Regular movement, even short walks or stretches, improves circulation, boosts brain oxygenation, and lifts your mood. Quality sleep acts as a performance booster by resetting the body's repair systems. Staying hydrated helps maintain concentration and stamina, preventing dehydration dips. And intentional recovery, including rest days, stretching, or relaxation techniques, is not laziness but a crucial part of maintaining sustained productivity.

Peak performers don't just manage hours; they manage energy cycles. They synchronize important tasks with their natural peaks in focus and creativity, whether those occur in the morning, afternoon, or evening. They take short recharge breaks to breathe, move, or reset their minds, ensuring mental sharpness stays consistent throughout the day. They also incorporate light movement every hour to fight physical stagnation and keep energy flowing.

Self-Care as a Leadership Essential

Your dedication to self-care isn't selfish; it's a mark of leadership. When you act from a state of emotional stability and physical energy, you make clearer, more confident decisions, set a positive example for others, and motivate those around you to prioritize their well-being. Strong leaders don't just achieve results; they demonstrate the behaviors that foster long-term success.

Consider how your current physical health impacts your energy and focus. Reflect on which emotions are the hardest for you to manage and how they influence your performance. Think about one self-care practice that, if practiced consistently, could improve your well-being right now.

Evaluate yourself in the following areas on a scale of 1-5

- Nutrition
- Movement
- Sleep Quality
- Stress Management
- Hydration
- Emotional Balance

Identify the one area where your score is lowest, then set a simple, achievable goal to improve over the next seven days. Track your progress and notice how small changes start to boost your energy and focus. Schedule time in your calendar for self-care, just as you would for essential meetings. This could be a peaceful walk in nature, preparing a nourishing meal, an evening of journaling, or a mid-week mindfulness break. Treat these self-care activities with the same importance as your professional commitments.

Chapter 9: Emotional & Physical Wellness for Peak Performance

1 Corinthians 6:19-20 (KJV) *What? know ye not that your body is the temple of the Holy Ghost which is in you, which ye have of God, and ye are not your own? For ye are bought with a price: therefore glorify God in your body, and in your spirit, which are God's.*

TED Talk:

Make Stress Your Friend – Kelly McGonigal

Further Reading Companion

- ⇒ *The Body Keeps the Score* – Dr. van der Kolk
- ⇒ *Eat Smarter* – Shawn Stevenson
- ⇒ *Boundaries* – Cloud & Townsend
- ⇒ *Burnout* – Nagoski Sisters
- ⇒ *Why We Sleep* – Dr. Matthew Walker

CHAPTER 10: BUILDING SUPPORT SYSTEMS & ACCOUNTABILITY CIRCLES

Surround yourself only with people who will lift you higher." — **Oprah Winfrey**

"*How you live your days reflects how you live your life.*"
— *Annie Dillard*

I've learned that no matter how self-disciplined or driven I am, I can't reach my full potential on my own. The people I surround myself with have a significant influence on my mindset and the rate of my progress. Sometimes, this impact is noticeable, like when a friend encourages me to keep going after I've stumbled. At other times, it's more subtle, such as realizing that being around people who are constantly working on self-improvement makes me want to do the same.

Achieving my personal best isn't just about willpower; it's about intentionally surrounding myself with people who inspire, challenge, and remind me of my goals when I'm tempted to forget them. These individuals help me stay consistent, motivated, and focused, even when life gets complicated.

I once heard Jim Rohn say that we are the average of the five people we spend the most time with. At first, I brushed it off as just another catchy phrase. But over the years, I've realized it's true. When I've been around groups where everyone is trying to grow, I've noticed myself working harder, thinking more clearly, and believing more in my abilities.

Being part of a growth-focused network means I'm surrounded by high standards, positive energy, and a culture where personal development is the norm. It also provides a space to find encouragement and practical advice when challenges arise. In these environments, I learn faster because I'm not figuring everything out on my own; I can benefit from others' experiences and insights.

Chapter 10: Building Support Systems & Accountability Circles

The opposite is also true. I've been in environments where negativity, gossip, and complacency were common. During those times, my energy and motivation slowly declined without me even noticing it. That's why I now carefully choose who I let influence my mindset and habits.

THE POWER OF ACCOUNTABILITY CIRCLES

An accountability circle is more than just a group of friends. It's a small, trusted team where we each commit to helping others follow through on their goals. I've been part of one for a while now, and I can honestly say it's one of the main reasons I stay consistent. When I know I must update the group on my progress, I'm much less likely to make excuses.

These circles have also shown me the power of different perspectives. Sometimes, I get stuck on a problem and can't see the way forward, but someone else in the group offers an idea I haven't thought of. They celebrate with me when I reach a milestone and remind me to keep going when I feel like quitting. Whether it's a mastermind group, a professional network, or just a few trusted friends, what matters most is that the circle is built on trust, respect, and a shared vision.

Building a dedicated support system has been a deliberate effort for me. It starts with finding people who are curious, motivated, and genuinely supportive. Sometimes I meet them at professional events or online communities. Other times, they are people I already know but haven't connected with on a deeper, growth-focused level.

I also value mentorship. Having someone who has already been where I want to go has helped me avoid unnecessary mistakes and inspired me to think more deeply than I would on my own. At the same time, I've learned that I need to be careful with my energy. There are people who, without meaning to drain my focus and motivation. Setting boundaries with those relationships has been just as important as building new ones.

I've noticed that accountability only works when it's mutual. In my own accountability partnerships, I make sure I am dependable, show up when I commit, listen

Chapter 10: Building Support Systems & Accountability Circles

without judgment, and provide honest yet supportive feedback.

I've realized that even small celebrations matter. A friend in my circle once said, "We don't wait for the big win to cheer; we cheer every step forward." That mindset helps keep momentum going. Sometimes, my most valuable contribution is simply being there and showing others they're not alone on their journey.

While friends and peers have greatly contributed to my growth, there have been moments when I needed a more structured approach to learning. That's when professional coaches and advisors come into play. The first time I worked with a coach, I was amazed at how quickly they identified patterns in my behavior that I couldn't see.

They didn't just motivate me; they offered frameworks, systems, and challenges that pushed me far beyond my comfort zone. Their perspective was entirely objective, which made their advice more precise and more focused. I now see investing in that kind of guidance as a way to take my own goals seriously.

ACHIEVING YOUR PERSONAL BEST: DAILY PRACTICES

I've come to believe that success isn't achieved in big leaps but through small, consistent steps taken every day. It's a quiet routine, including activities like morning planning, regular reflection, and steady follow-throughs, which lead to real progress.

I rely on simple tools to stay on course. For example, I keep a daily journal where I record my focus for the day, wins, and lessons learned. My mornings begin with a routine that helps me feel centered. Sometimes it's a quick meditation, a walk, or just reviewing my priorities. In the evening, I spend a few minutes reflecting on how I showed up that day and where I can improve tomorrow. Over time, these habits have created a rhythm that keeps me progressing.

I've learned that my personal best doesn't happen alone. It's made with the help of others who lift me up and keep me focused. A strong, intentional network motivates me to reach higher. Accountability groups keep me consistent. Professional guidance sharpens my skills. And daily practices, repeated with care, lay the

Chapter 10: Building Support Systems & Accountability Circles

groundwork for long-term success. By nurturing my relationships and fully engaging in them, I've built a support system that makes achieving my personal best not just possible but unavoidable.

Chapter 10: Building Support Systems & Accountability Circles

Proverbs 27:17 (KJV) *Iron sharpeneth iron; so a man sharpeneth the countenance of his friend.*

TED Talk:

The Power of Peer Support – Noudvan Hecke

Further Reading Companion

- ⇒ *The Power of Who* – Bob Beaudine
- ⇒ *Find Your People* – Jennie Allen
- ⇒ *Relational Intelligence* – Dharius Daniels
- ⇒ *Tribe* – Sebastian Junger
- ⇒ *Who Not How* – Dan Sullivan

CHAPTER 11:
LEADING WITH PURPOSE & AUTHENTICITY

"Be yourself; everyone else is already taken." — **Oscar Wilde**

Authentic leadership isn't determined by the title on your business card or how many followers you have. It's about the influence you create, the impact you leave behind, and the authenticity you show. As you develop into your personal best, leadership opportunities often come naturally, not because you chase after them, but because your growth inspires others to rise with you.

Leading with authenticity means acting with honesty, clarity, and compassion. It involves showing up as your true self, aligning your actions with your values, and inspiring others to do the same. Leadership based on authenticity is steady and strong because it's rooted in truth, not just performance.

Achieving personal success is highly rewarding, but it's true value depends on how you use it. Purposeful leadership guides your growth by uplifting others, supporting meaningful causes, and creating ripple effects that go far beyond your own goals. The most influential leaders lead by example, inspire others to chase their own version of excellence, and prioritize service, contribution, and collective success over personal recognition. Leadership isn't a final point; it's an ongoing wave of influence.

LEADING YOURSELF FIRST

The core of exceptional leadership is self-leadership. Before guiding others, you need to hold yourself to the same standards you expect from them. This involves practicing self-accountability, managing your emotions, especially under pressure, and being open about your goals and why they matter.

Leading yourself effectively means understanding your core values and evaluating your actions based on them.

It involves tracking your commitments and reliably following through. It also requires reflecting on how well your daily choices align with your larger mission. Self-discipline, emotional intelligence, and a strong internal compass form the foundation of this process.

Reflect on this: How do you hold yourself accountable for your personal and professional goals? Which emotional trigger most often disrupts your focus or presence? What values are non-negotiable in how you live and lead? Your answers to these questions will reveal the quality of your self-leadership.

Authenticity is your leadership superpower. It takes courage to embrace your unique strengths, values, and personality rather than bending to meet external expectations. Authentic leaders are open and honest in their communication. They admit to mistakes, embrace vulnerability, and ensure their actions align with their words. This consistency builds trust, and trust is the foundation of leadership.

When you lead authentically, you create an environment where others feel safe to do the same. This openness fosters innovation, teamwork, and a shared sense of belonging.

Purpose fuels long-term leadership. It gives meaning to your work and helps you stay motivated through challenges. To find your leadership purpose, consider the kind of impact you want to have on others, the values that influence your decisions, and the legacy you hope to leave behind.

From there, craft a clear leadership purpose statement. For example, *I lead with compassion and integrity. My purpose is to empower others to reach their highest potential. I will build a legacy of courage, kindness, and meaningful impact.* Keep this statement visible and let it guide your daily actions.

THE POWER OF SERVANT LEADERSHIP

Servant leadership challenges traditional leadership methods. Instead of emphasizing authority and control, it centers on serving others, providing support, encouraging teamwork, and fostering environments where people can succeed. This leadership style values personal growth and well-being, listens with empathy, shares credit freely, and creates safe spaces for people to excel.

When you lead by serving, you inspire loyalty, foster trust, and create high-performing communities.

In today's connected world, leadership extends beyond boardrooms and official titles. Every interaction, whether face-to-face, online, or in your local community, offers a chance to lead. You influence others through your words, actions, and attitudes.

Reflect on your daily interactions: What message are you sending? How are you using your influence, no matter how small, to uplift and inspire? Often, the most impactful leadership happens in everyday moments. Small, consistent acts of authenticity and encouragement can create ripple effects far beyond what you see.

One way to improve your leadership is to identify your top three leadership values, such as integrity, growth, and service, and regularly evaluate how well your actions align with them. Set aside time each week for reflection to review your self-leadership and make any necessary adjustments.

Affirmations for Purposeful and Authentic Leadership

I lead myself with integrity, clarity, and purpose. I inspire others through my genuine actions and words. My leadership reflects my true self, not my title. Each day, I create waves of positive influence through service and sincerity. I am a leader who earns trust, encourages growth, and lifts others.

Leadership is about influence, not just position, and authenticity boosts that influence. As you shift from pursuing personal success to serving with purpose, remember that leading yourself first builds the foundation for effectively guiding others. Servant leadership cultivates empowered, high-performing communities. No matter your title or role, your platform is always large enough to create a meaningful impact when you lead with integrity and purpose.

Chapter 11: Leading with Purpose & Authenticity

Micah 6:8 (KJV) He hath shewed thee, O man, what is good; and what doth the LORD require of thee, but to do justly, and to love mercy, and to walk humbly with thy God?

TED Talk:

Everyday Leadership – Drew Dudley

Further Reading Companion

- ⇒ *The Leader Who Had No Title* – Robin Sharma
- ⇒ *Lead from the Outside* – Stacey Abrams
- ⇒ *Dare to Lead* – Brené Brown
- ⇒ *The Purpose Driven Life* – Rick Warren
- ⇒ *Leadership and the New Science* – Margaret Wheatley
- ⇒ *Realizing Your Public Service Potential: Empowering Career Strategies for Tomorrow's Change-Makers* – Leben, Deborah

CHAPTER 12: ACHIEVING YOUR PERSONAL BEST: A LIFELONG JOURNEY

"Success is not a destination, but the road that you're on."
—*Marlon Wayans*

Achieving your personal best isn't about hitting a final milestone. It's a lifelong journey of growth, curiosity, and contribution. Each achievement you reach opens new possibilities, enhances self-awareness, and expands your sphere of influence. The person you are today is just a glimpse of who you can become. As you grow, your ideas of success, fulfillment, and legacy will evolve with you. There is no fixed version of yourself, only wiser, more impactful versions waiting to emerge.

Chapter 12: Achieving Your Personal Best: A Lifelong Journey

SUCCESS AS AN EVOLVING TARGET

One of the biggest myths about success is that it's a fixed point. In reality, goals that once felt like mountains to climb will eventually become your new normal. Your skills, experiences, and perspectives will evolve your ambitions over time. Every season of life encourages you to rethink what "your personal best" means. Instead of chasing a fixed idea of success, a more positive approach is to embrace ongoing growth and reinvention as a core part of who you are.

CELEBRATING PROGRESS, NOT JUST OUTCOMES

In the pursuit of excellence, it's tempting to focus on the future, always aiming for the next achievement without taking a moment to appreciate the progress already made. However, real growth lies in small, daily victories, the consistent habits you build, the mindset shifts you make, and the quiet resilience you show when faced with obstacles. When you celebrate progress, you strengthen your identity as someone dedicated to growth, boost your motivation to keep improving, and cultivate a deep sense of gratitude for the journey itself.

Success isn't just the moment you reach a destination; it's also the person you become along the way.

Lifelong Learning: Staying Relevant and Vital

In a world that changes rapidly, lifelong learning is essential for staying energized, adaptable, and impactful. Lifelong learners view each day as an opportunity to expand their knowledge, refine their skills, and deepen their understanding of the world. This includes setting deliberate learning goals, seeking mentorship and guidance, periodically revisiting and refining your personal vision, and remaining curious. It also involves listening to feedback without defensiveness, exploring innovative ideas openly, and allowing change to shape you into a stronger, wiser person. Learning throughout your life is the energy that keeps your journey vibrant.

Building a Legacy Through Daily Intentionality

Legacy isn't built on dramatic, isolated moments; it's shaped through small, consistent choices you make every day. It appears in how you support others, the values you uphold, and the ripple effect you create on

Chapter 12: Achieving Your Personal Best: A Lifelong Journey

those around you. Consider what you want to be remembered for, the values your daily actions demonstrate, and the people affected by your growth. Legacy isn't something you leave behind when you pass away; it's something you live each day.

BECOMING A LIFELONG ACHIEVER

Growth is never accidental; it demands intentional action and ongoing dedication. Identify a skill that excites and challenges you, and commit to developing it. Choose one habit that keeps you grounded in daily excellence and protect it fiercely. Create a feedback loop, whether through journaling, digital tracking, or regular check-ins with someone you trust, to observe your progress in real time. Consistent self-awareness and purposeful effort will ensure you keep moving forward.

REFLECTION FOR THE ROAD AHEAD

Pause and reflect: How has your definition of "personal best" evolved during this journey? Which activities make you lose track of time because they energize and motivate you? Which causes or issues speak to your heart so deeply that they demand your involvement?

And most importantly, how will you ensure your growth continues long after the final page of this book?

ACTION FOR SUSTAINED GROWTH

Start by drafting your personal purpose statement. In one sentence, define your core mission. In another, explain how you plan to contribute to others. In a third, share the legacy you hope to create through your daily choices. Then, establish three learning goals for the year; ambitious goals that push your abilities and fit with your evolving vision. Find someone who can hold you accountable, whether a mentor, peer, or trusted friend, and agree on regular check-ins to review your progress. Finally, challenge yourself to embody your purpose practically each week through your conversations, actions, and service.

You are not here to lead an ordinary life. You are here to rise, grow, and inspire others. Your personal best isn't a destination; it's a daily decision, a lifelong journey, and a legacy you're creating. The best version of yourself is always ahead of you, and each morning offers a new opportunity to start fresh.

Chapter 12: Achieving Your Personal Best: A Lifelong Journey

Philippians 3:13–14 (KJV) Brethren, I count not myself to have apprehended: but this one thing I do, forgetting those things which are behind, and reaching forth unto those things which are before, I press toward the mark for the prize of the high calling of God in Christ Jesus.

TED Talk:

The Power of Yet – Carol Dweck

Further Reading Companion

- ⇒ *The Infinite Game* – Simon Sinek
- ⇒ *The Compound Effect* – Darren Hardy
- ⇒ *Becoming* – Michelle Obama
- ⇒ *The Traveler's Gift* – Andy Andrews
- ⇒ *15 Laws of Growth* – John Maxwell

www.ingramcontent.com/pod-product-compliance
Lightning Source LLC
Chambersburg PA
CBHW022056090426
42743CB00028B/538